God Knows Me From A - Z

A Call-and-Response Alphabet Book for Littles

Vivian Adam

ADAM
COLLECTIVE
PUBLISHING

Published by
Adam Collective Publishing
An imprint of Adam Strategy Collective, LLC

ISBN: 979-8-9957895-1-2
First Edition

Illustrations were created and designed using digital creative tools and curated by the author.

Photo editing and post-production by JAO Pictures
www.jaopictures.com

Scripture references are used for inspirational and educational purposes only. No direct biblical
text is quoted.

This book is intended to encourage faith and positive identity in children and is not a substitute
for parental guidance, pastoral care, or professional advice.

Printed in the United States of America

For more information, visit www.theadamcollective.com

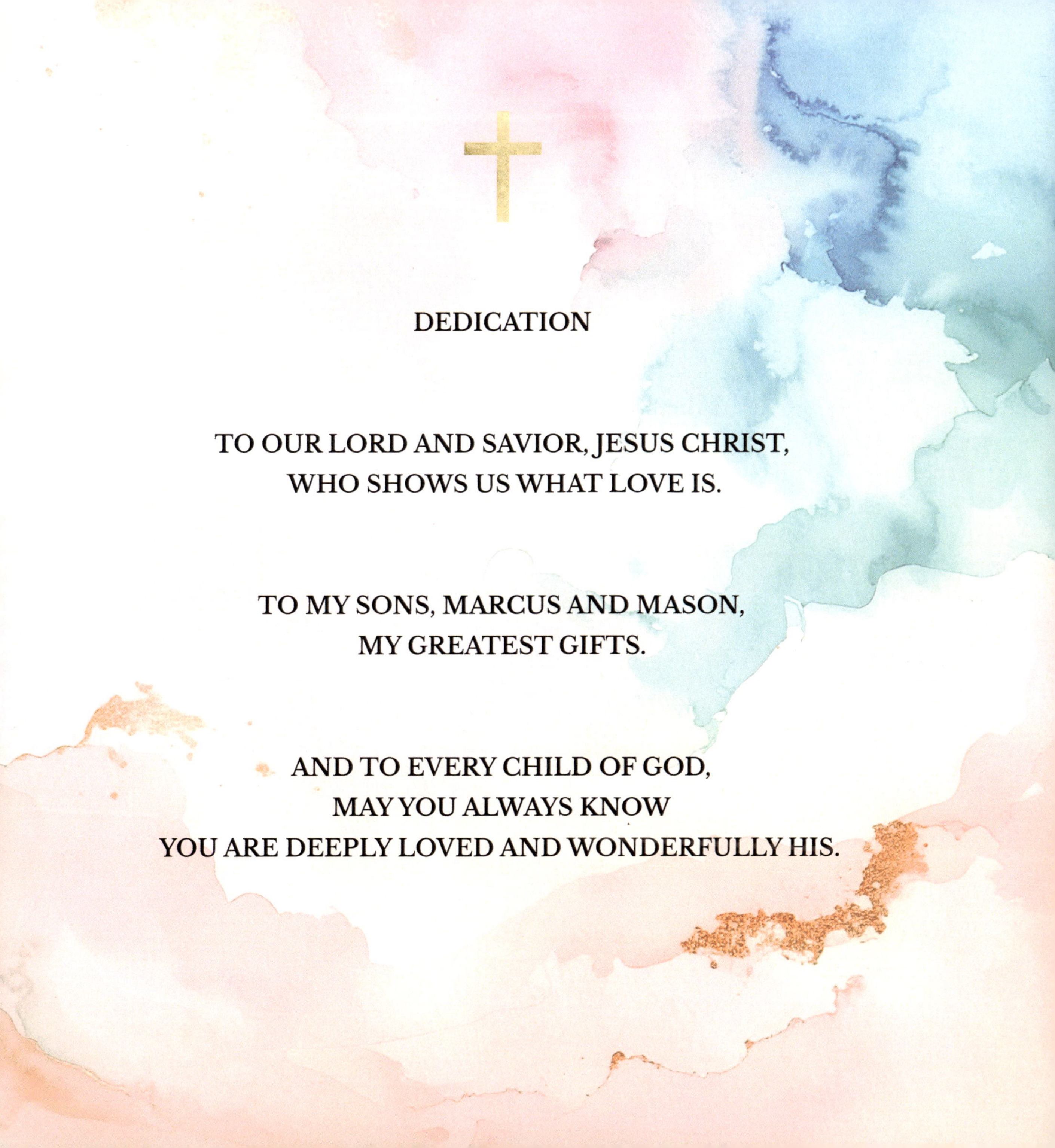

DEDICATION

TO OUR LORD AND SAVIOR, JESUS CHRIST,
WHO SHOWS US WHAT LOVE IS.

TO MY SONS, MARCUS AND MASON,
MY GREATEST GIFTS.

AND TO EVERY CHILD OF GOD,
MAY YOU ALWAYS KNOW
YOU ARE DEEPLY LOVED AND WONDERFULLY HIS.

Intro (For Parents & Caregivers)

Why Speaking Identity Matters

Children begin learning who they are long before they can explain it. The words they hear repeated often become the truths they believe about themselves.

When we speak God's truth over our children, we help shape their hearts with confidence, security, and faith. Instead of defining themselves by feelings, mistakes, or the opinions of others, they begin to understand who they are through God's unchanging love.

This book is designed to help you speak biblical identity aloud—simply and consistently. As you read together, your child hears the beautiful truth of who God says they are.

How to Use This Book

Read the sentence stem aloud (for example: "God says I am...")

Pause and let your child repeat the last word.

Keep it slow, joyful, and pressure-free.

Even if your child doesn't repeat the words right away, their heart is still listening.

May these words plant seeds of truth in your child's heart that will grow for a lifetime.

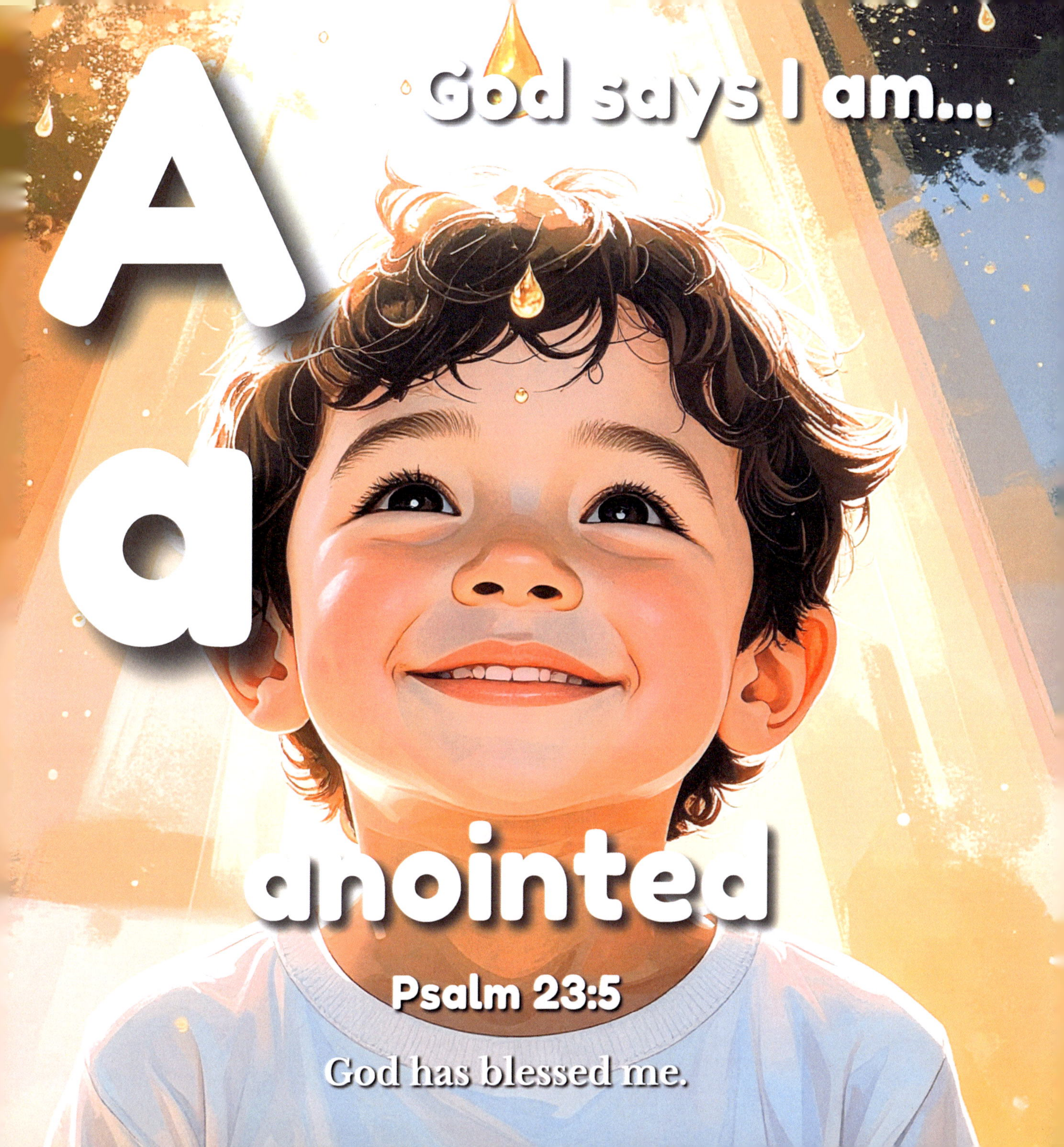
God says I am...
A a
anointed
Psalm 23:5
God has blessed me.

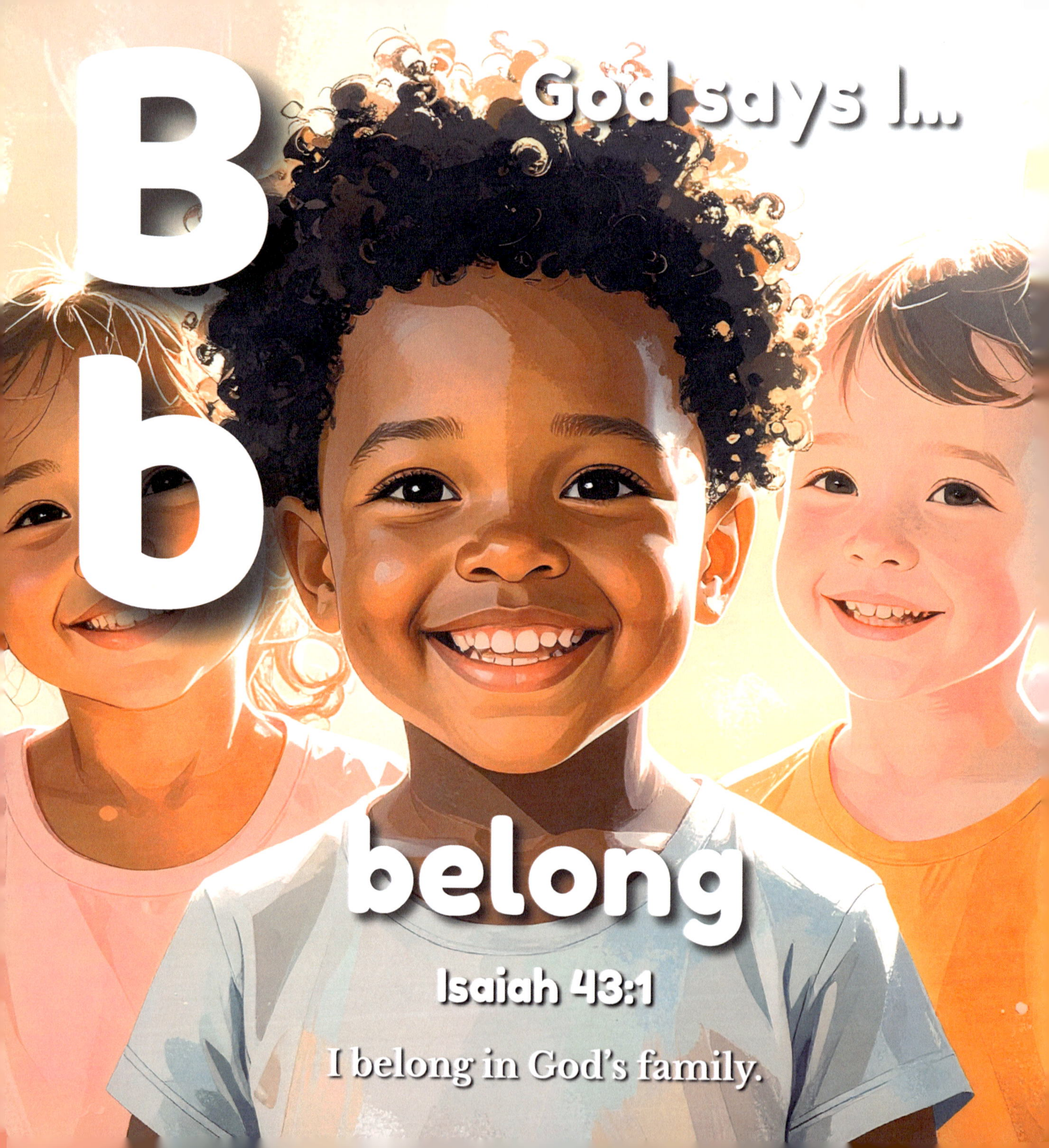

B b
God says I...
belong
Isaiah 43:1
I belong in God's family.

God says I am...
C c
chosen
1 Peter 2:9
God picked me on purpose.

Dd
God says I am His...
delight
Zephaniah 3:17
God smiles when He looks at me.

God says I am...
Enough
enough
2 Corinthians 12:9
I am just right the way I am.

F f
God says I am...
fearfully and wonderfully made.
Psalm 139:14
God made me special and wonderful.

God says I am a...
G
g
gift
Psalm 127:3
I am a special gift from God.

H h
God says I am...
holy
1 Peter 1:15
I am set apart for God.

God says I am...
I
important
Matthew 6:26
I matter to God.

J j
God says I am...
joyful
Nehemiah 8:10
God's love makes me happy.

God says I am...
K k
known
Jeremiah 1:5
God knows all about me.

God says I am...
I
loved
Jeremiah 31:3
God loves me very much.

M m
God says I am...
made in His image
Genesis 1:27
God made me to be like Him.

N
n
God says I am...
never alone
Hebrews 13:5
God is always with me.

God says I am an...
overcomer
Romans 8:37
With God's help, I can do hard things.

P p
God says I have a...
purpose
Jeremiah 29:11
God has a plan for me.

God says I am...
Q q
quick to listen
James 1:19
I listen carefully and do what God says.

God says I am...
R r
redeemed
Ephesians 1:7
Jesus chose me and brought me close to God.

S
s
God says I am...
strong
Ephesians 6:10
God helps me be brave and strong.

God says I am...
T t
treasured
Deuteronomy 7:6
I am precious to God.

U u
God says I am...
united with Him
1 Corinthians 6:17
I stay close to Jesus.

God says I am...
victorious
1 Corinthians 15:57
God helps me win over fear.

W
W
God says I am...
watched over
Psalm 121:5
God keeps me safe.

God says I am...
eXtra special
Ephesians 2:10
God knew the world needed one of me.

Y
y
God says I am a child of...
Yahweh
1 John 3:1
I am God's child.

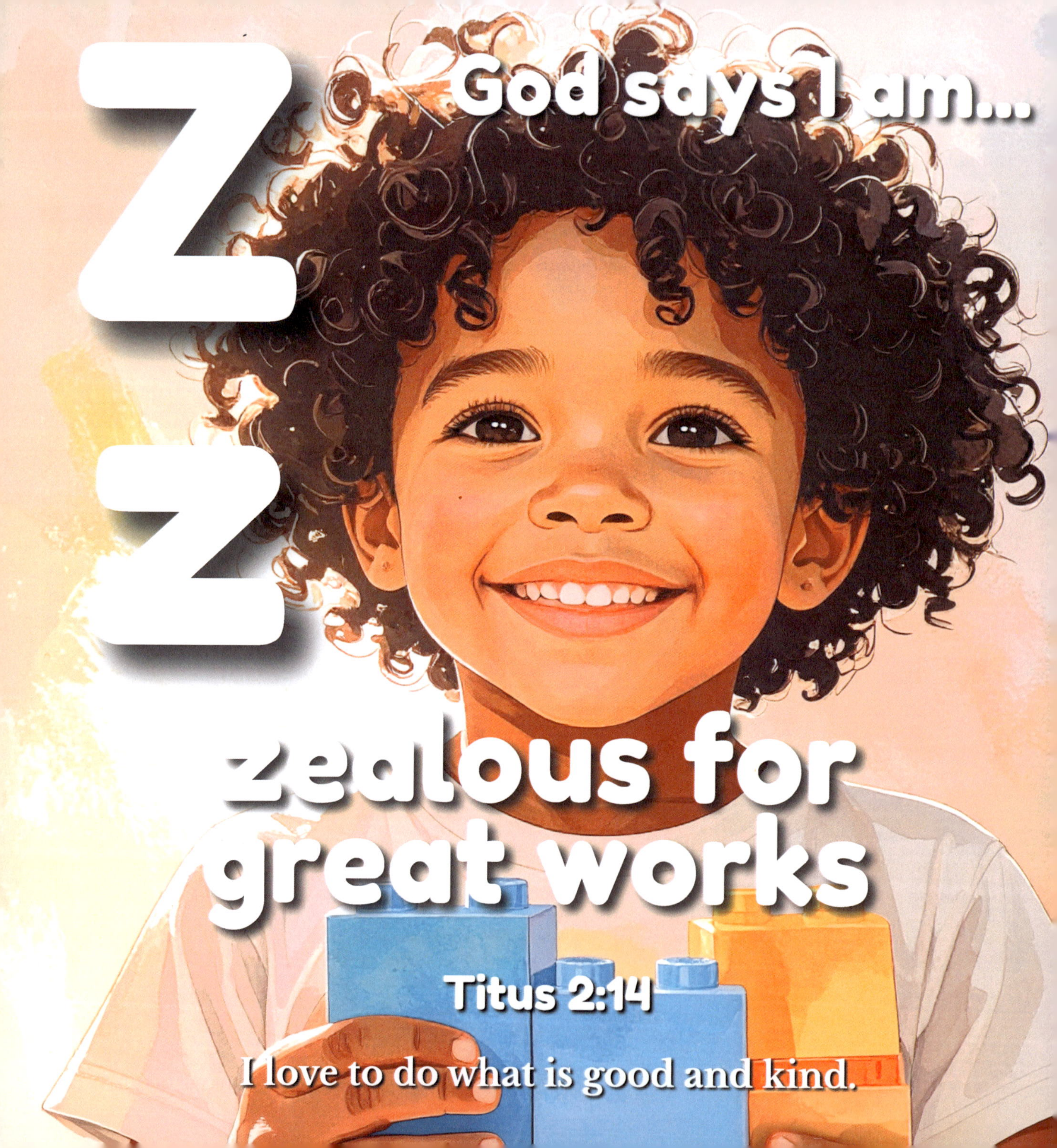

Z
z
God says I am...
zealous for great works
Titus 2:14
I love to do what is good and kind.